NEVER THE SAME: Encounters with Jesus

NEVER THE SAME:
Encounters with Jesus

Jacquelin McCall Brown
Xulon Press

Xulon Press
2301 Lucien Way #415
Maitland, FL 32751
407.339.4217
www.xulonpress.com

© 2017 by Jacquelin McCall Brown

All rights reserved solely by the author. The author guarantees all contents are original and do not infringe upon the legal rights of any other person or work. No part of this book may be reproduced in any form without the permission of the author. The views expressed in this book are not necessarily those of the publisher.

Scripture quotations taken from the Holy Bible, New International Version (NIV). Copyright © 1973, 1978, 1984, 2011 by Biblica, Inc.™. Used by permission. All rights reserved.

Edited by Xulon Press.

Printed in the United States of America.

ISBN-13: 9781545616895

CONTENTS

Dedication..................................ix

Introduction................................xi

PART I

Mother's Day (Luke 1:26-2:7) 3

Worth the Wait (Luke 2:25-28) 6

More than Cousins (Mark 1:1-11) 9

An Unlikely Witness (John 4:1-42).............. 12

Trust and Obey (John 4:46-53) 17

Three Powerful Words (John 11:1-44) 20

Seeing Jesus (Matthew 9:27-31)................ 24

Blind Trust (John 9:1-7) 27

Blind Trust: Part 2 (John 9:8-34) 30

The Secret Admirer (John 3:1-21; 7:50-51;

    19:39-40)...............................34

Whatever It Takes (Mark 10:46-47;
   Luke 18:35-43) 38

An Attitude of Gratitude (Luke 17:11-19) 41

Dying to Meet Jesus (Luke 7:11-17). 45

Stand Up For Jesus (Luke 5:17-26) 48

Touching Jesus (Mark 5:24-34) 52

Falling at the Feet of Jesus (Luke 8:40-56) 55

Death Sentence (John 8:1-11). 59

Don't Lose Hope (John 5:1-18) 64

More Than Enough (Matthew 14:13-21) 68

Saving the Best for Last (John 2:1-11) 72

No Ordinary Day (Matthew 27:51-54) 77

A Congregation of Two (Luke 24:13-35) 81

PART II

"Somebody Call 9-1-1" (Jeremiah 29:11) 87

The Waiting Game (Isaiah 30:18). 90

What a Friend (Proverbs 18:24) 94

Testimony of Healing (2 Kings 20:5) 98

PART III

The "Ultimate" Encounter (Ephesians 2:8-9) 109

DEDICATION

My life has been filled with special people who have inspired me and made me the person I am today. This book is dedicated to them.

First are my daughters, Jennifer and Jessica. As I have had the privilege of watching you grow from birth to two incredible, talented, young women, I am so thankful that God blessed me to be your mama. I am so proud of you both and love you dearly.

Next is the memory of my sweet mother, Florence. Her inspiration and encouragement have made an incredible difference in my life. Her sense of humor was contagious; and I literally owe my life to her (more on that later). I only wish she were here today to vicariously share in the excitement of publishing my first book.

I also dedicate this book to my husband, Jim. Your unconditional love for me reflects Christ's love for the Church. You believed in me when no one else did, and for that I am forever grateful. You are my best friend and the love of my life.

Last, but definitely not least, this book is dedicated to my Lord and Savior Jesus Christ. Without His presence in my life, this book could not have been written.

INTRODUCTION

Simeon and Anna, Mary the Mother of Jesus, John the Baptist, Lazarus, the Roman centurion and the Samaritan woman: what do these, and countless others, have in common? Each of them has a story to tell. Within that story, we find that many times they specifically reached out to Jesus; more importantly, He reached out to them.

At some point in their lives, each of them had an *"encounter"* with Jesus Christ, the Son of God.

Regardless of where you may be in life, it is my heartfelt prayer that as you ponder the adventures of this biblical cast of characters, you will come to the realization, as I have, that an encounter with Jesus is ***life-changing***. For once a person encounters Jesus, he/she is forever changed.

In other words, he/she is NEVER THE SAME.

To God Be the Glory.

PART 1

MOTHER'S DAY

One of life's greatest blessings and gifts from God is to be a mother. From the instant a woman realizes she is carrying another life within her until that joyful moment when her baby is born, a woman can have no greater experience in her life, apart from salvation.

The Bible tells us that Mary was a woman who found favor with God (Luke 1:30). What a privilege to know God, and equally a privilege to know His son firsthand!

Still, I find it difficult to imagine how Mary must have felt when the angel Gabriel visited her with the unexpected news of being chosen to be the mother of the Messiah, the promised Savior and Son of God. I can picture how most women, including myself, would react if something so daunting happened to us: "*Really,*

*Gabriel? You've **got** to be kidding! God has chosen me to do **what**?"*

In today's world, being unmarried and pregnant doesn't seem to carry the shame and stigma that it was in the time of Mary. Back in those days, a woman finding herself in that precarious position would be considered an outcast; she would be a disgrace to her family and could even face death. She would, no doubt, be devastated beyond words.

Yet, we know that this is not the way Mary's story played out. In her quiet and gentle spirit, I can almost hear Mary say to Gabriel, *"I am the Lord's servant. May it be to me as you have said"* (Luke 1:38). As Mary's story continues, we find her visiting her cousin Elizabeth, who also was with child. Upon hearing Mary's voice, Elizabeth was "filled with the Holy Spirit", as Elizabeth's baby "leaped in her womb" (Luke 1:41).

We find Mary glorifying and praising God for this miracle of life. She tells Elizabeth that *"He has done great things for me—holy is his name"* (Luke 1:46-55).

Mary *was* blessed to experience Jesus, to encounter Jesus and to know Him for His entire life. As we read in the Scriptures, the birth, death and subsequent resurrection of Jesus would forever change her life. She would never be the same.

While we may not be asked by God to do anything quite as spectacular as being the mother of Jesus, so many times God places situations and people in our lives for a specific reason or task. Instead of questioning God when those circumstances occur, we need to reflect a spirit like Mary's.

May we remember that God will never assign us a task for which He has not first equipped us; and may we, like Mary, find it easy to respond to God's call in a way that blesses Him, as well as those around us.

WORTH THE WAIT

Impatience; we've all experienced it.

Perhaps it's being placed on hold for an indefinite amount of time when trying to reach someone by telephone. Maybe it's the bumper-to-bumper traffic and the brake lights on the myriad vehicles in front of us, which seems to stretch on for miles. Perhaps it's that unbelievably long checkout line at the grocery store, moving at a snail's pace; or maybe our internet provider is just not fast enough.

Webster's Dictionary defines being impatient as "lacking patience; specifically annoyed because of delay, opposition; restlessly eager to do something."[1] In today's world, we seem to be in such a hurry all the time. We **do** lack patience; we **do** tend to get annoyed

---

[1] <u>Webster's New World Dictionary and Thesaurus</u>, Second Edition, Wiley Publishing, 2002, P. 318.

easily. We rush through our everyday lives and absolutely **don't** want to wait for anything.

Or anyone.

Such was not the case with two elderly warriors of the faith, Simeon and Anna.

Can you just imagine living every day of your life with the expectation and anticipation that before your life was over, you would meet the Messiah face to face? This was the promise revealed to Simeon by the Holy Spirit.

As was the custom in those days, Joseph and Mary took Jesus to Jerusalem to present Him to God, a baby dedication if you will (Luke 2:27-28). The Bible tells us that as Simeon took Jesus in his arms and gazed upon the face of baby Jesus for the first time, he immediately recognized that this child was more than just a baby; he recognized the true identity of Jesus and gave God praise for allowing him to see the Promised One.

I can just picture this elderly saint holding Jesus and expressing such a profound (and perhaps loud) praise to God that another warrior of the faith, a prophetess named Anna, couldn't help but overhear all the commotion. Approaching Mary and Joseph, Anna also expressed praise and thanks to God for allowing her to see the fulfillment of His promised Messiah, the "redemption of Jerusalem" (Luke 2:38).

You see, after meeting Jesus, Simeon and Anna were never the same.

What an incredible blessing this encounter with Jesus must have been to them! The remainder of their days must have been so precious. If you were to ask Simeon and Anna if that encounter with Jesus was worth waiting a lifetime, their response would be a resounding *"YES!"*

Getting back to the topic of impatience, we need to ask ourselves why we so easily sweat the small stuff in our lives. Does this situation we're getting upset about even begin to compare with the lifetime wait of those two elderly saints?

May God help us to keep things in proper perspective. When we feel that sudden twinge of impatience creeping into our thoughts, may we be reminded of Simeon and Anna; two elderly saints who patiently waited their entire lives for the fulfillment of God's promise: an encounter with Jesus.

MORE THAN COUSINS

John the Baptist was the son of Elizabeth, a cousin to Mary, the mother of Jesus. Being cousins, one could surmise that John and Jesus must have spent plenty of time together playing as children, as they grew in stature. They were relatives and obviously knew one another very well.

The Bible tells us that God gave John a very important task—to be the forerunner of God's son: to preach the message of repentance from sin; to prepare the people for the coming Savior. John's message to the people was this: *"After me will come one more powerful than I, the thongs of whose sandals I am not worthy to stoop down and untie. I baptize you with water, but he will baptize you with the Holy Spirit"* (John 1:7-8).

We learn that as a result of his preaching, the whole Judean countryside and all the people of Jerusalem went out to hear John's message, and to be baptized with water as a sign of their repentance.

Then Jesus arrived on the scene.

It was at that moment that the bond between these two men dramatically changed. When John baptized Jesus and saw the Holy Spirit descending from heaven as a dove, and heard a voice from heaven saying, *"You are my Son whom I love; with you I am well pleased"* (Mark 1:10-11), John received the revelation from God who Jesus really was...the Son of God and promised Messiah. John's head knowledge of Jesus quickly became heart knowledge. Suddenly, John realized that he and Jesus were much more than cousins; they were partners in ministry.

The baptism of Jesus marked the beginning of Jesus' public ministry; it also marked the gradual decline of John's ministry. In fact, John said, *"He must become greater; I must become less"* (John 3:30). Yet, I can't help but believe that John the Baptist's encounter with Jesus surely must have stirred his spirit to even greater heights. His final days of ministry must have been filled with such zeal and fervor to preach the good news of Jesus Christ.

It is safe to say that from that dramatic encounter with Jesus at the Jordan River, John's life and ministry were never the same.

As we meditate upon the story of John the Baptist, may God also reveal to us who Jesus is, and renew our hearts and minds with a freshness of spirit. May our prayer reflect the words of Psalm 51:10, 12: *"Create in me a pure heart, O God, and renew a steadfast spirit within me. Restore to me the joy of your salvation and grant me a willing spirit, to sustain me."*

AN UNLIKELY WITNESS

The dictionary defines a witness as "one who saw, or can give a firsthand account of something".[2]

As followers of Jesus, the Bible exhorts us to be His witnesses *"to the ends of the earth"* (Acts 1:8). Simply put, Christ has instructed us to share the good news of the gospel with those around us. Whether it be to neighbors in our local community, our co-workers or simple strangers we happen to come in contact with, the idea is that we are to witness to others who may not have a personal relationship and saving knowledge of Jesus Christ.

We are not called to be mere "pew warmers" from week to week, but we have been called to spread God's message of love and forgiveness to those whom God

---

[2] Webster's New World Dictionary and Thesaurus, Second Edition, Wiley Publishing, 2002, P. 730.

has placed in our lives. We are to share the good news of John 3:16-17 to others: *"For God so loved the world that he gave his one and only Son, that whoever believes in him shall not perish but have eternal life. For God did not send his Son into the world to condemn the world, but to save the world through him."*

Is there such a thing as a typical witness? As we think about someone witnessing for Jesus, whom do we tend to focus on? Someone who has been a believer for a very long time; someone who is well-versed in the Bible; someone who is spiritually mature? Isn't that the type of person who will win others to Christ?

Yet in the Gospel of John, chapter 4, we are confronted with the story of a very unlikely witness; someone with a poor reputation and very low standing in her community.

A sinner.

We're talking about the Samaritan woman, often referred to as the "woman at the well".

Of all the most obvious candidates, she is certainly not the one you would choose to win others to Christ; but as we read the narrative in John 4:1-42, that is exactly what we find.

Jesus, tired and thirsty from His long journey, finds a place to rest near a well in Samaria. When this Samaritan woman arrives on the scene, Jesus begins a conversation with her, asking her for a drink of water from the well. Her reaction to Jesus is one of surprise, as the traditions of biblical history of that time dictated that Jews and Samaritans did not associate with one another.

Note she is not just any Samaritan woman; she is lower than low, and her reputation is stained with scandalous sins: five failed marriages and currently living in adultery with a man who is not her husband. Wondering why Jesus was conversing with her, she questions him.

Jesus and His captive audience of one are speaking on two different levels.

The Samaritan woman, unable to perceive that Jesus is talking about spiritual thirst rather than physical thirst, reminds Him that He doesn't have anything to draw water from this deep well. Jesus responds by telling her that if she only knew who He was, He would have given her living water and she would never thirst again.

As their conversation continues, Jesus reveals to the Samaritan woman that He knows all about her past. He also reveals to her that He is the Messiah.

AN UNLIKELY WITNESS

This revelation must have really shaken up the Samaritan woman as she immediately returns to town, leaving her water jar behind.

She is on a mission.

She now has a testimony.

This encounter with Jesus has changed her life.

The Bible tells us that *"Many of the Samaritans from that town believed in Jesus because of that woman's testimony"* (John 4:39).

Reading further in this passage, we learn that the Samaritans came to Jesus, invited Him to say with them for a few days and, *"because of his words, many more became believers"* (John 4:40-41).

Following her encounter with Jesus, the life of this Samaritan woman was never the same.

Although she may have appeared to be an unlikely witness for Christ, her encounter with Jesus resulted in many people becoming believers.

May the story of this Samaritan woman serve to remind us that regardless of our pasts or present circumstances, God can use us for His purposes and His glory. May it encourage us to realize that God can use anyone in any station of life to be His witnesses. May we remember that it's not who we are or what we have done, but what He can accomplish through us that truly matters.

TRUST AND OBEY

Not long after His encounter at the well with the Samaritan woman, we find Jesus returning to Cana in Galilee, the site of His first miracle. It is here where a government official makes his way, some twenty miles, specifically to find Jesus. In fact, the Bible tells us that this royal official went to Jesus and *"begged him to come and heal his son, who was close to death"* (John 4:47).

Being a parent, I can just imagine the anguish this father was experiencing in those brief moments as he approached Jesus. Sensing this man's devastation, but also his great faith, we find Jesus instructing this man to go home; *"Your son will live"* (John 4:50).

As we read this passage in the Gospel of John, it's so easy to simply take this account at face value; after all, it's about someone else. It doesn't affect anything in *our* personal lives. We may reason, "If Jesus said it, of course the man's son will be healed."

Let's be honest for a moment: how many of us in a similar situation, when told to go home, would do so without questioning Jesus?

Would we be persistent and try to convince Jesus that He should do things the way we suggest, that He *needs* to come with us and heal our son? Remember, up until this point, the only miracle we've seen or heard about was when Jesus turned water into wine, and He was there in person when that miracle occurred.

What would we say to Jesus to convince Him? "Really, Jesus? Are you kidding me? Just go home?" Or try to rationalize with Jesus: "I don't think you realize the gravity of my situation. My son is SICK. We're not talking about a summer cold here…we're talking deathbed sick!"

Or would we be like the royal official, taking Jesus at His word, and immediately, obediently begin the long journey back home? In other words, would we place our trust in Jesus and believe His words to be true?

Just ask the royal official.

While on his way homeward, he was met by one of his servants who shared the good news of the royal official's son being healed (John 4:51-52). This incredible miracle not only caused the man's son to be healed, but the Bible tells us that it caused *the entire household* to believe.

In other words, the lives of an entire family were immediately changed due to the faith of this father; both physical and spiritual healing took place that day. From that moment forward, the household of this royal official was never the same.

As we reflect on this one man's faith, may we be willing to take Jesus at His word. May we trust Him with the lives and well-being of our children, and leave them in the good hands of a Savior who cares.

THREE POWERFUL WORDS

Ever felt disappointed?
Discouraged?

Like your best friend abandoned you in your hour of need?

Just ask Mary and Martha.

Their brother, Lazarus, was very ill; in fact, he was on his deathbed. They knew Jesus could heal him, so they sent word to Jesus, *"Lord, the one you love is sick"* (John 11:3). The first time you hear this account in a sermon, or read it in the Bible, your basic instinct and thoughts are "Yes, send for Jesus. He can heal Lazarus."

Yet, we know this is NOT what happens.

After the messenger finds Jesus and informs Him of Lazarus' condition, we find that Jesus does not immediately return to Bethany. Somehow, this urgent request of these two sisters appears to go unnoticed by Jesus. We know it wasn't a few hours, or even one or two days before Jesus returns; in fact, it is three days.

Three LONG days.

Lazarus has now died.

This story seems to have a different twist than the other miracles of Jesus. It may well be the only narrative account where Jesus performs a miracle without any apparent sense of urgency. Have you ever wondered why Jesus lingered?

Did Jesus not realize how ill his dear friend Lazarus was? Did He know that by the time He arrived back in Bethany that Lazarus would have been dead for three days? Did He not care how heartbroken and grief-stricken Mary and Martha would be? Or how disappointed Lazarus must have been as he breathed his last breath, hoping and praying that Jesus would come to his rescue and perform a healing miracle?

Rest assured that Jesus was fully aware of Lazarus' deathbed condition. He may have seemed indifferent to ministering to his friend, Lazarus, but nothing could be further from the truth. What it all comes down to is this: whether Lazarus was dead one hour, one day, one week or one year, it did not matter.

He was dead.

We read that when Jesus arrived at the tomb of Lazarus, He was so overcome with grief that He wept (John 11:35). He knew that God was about to receive glory in the midst of this tragedy; yet the humanness of Jesus comes through. As tears begin to fall down His cheeks, the compassion of Jesus experiencing this great loss seems to overwhelm Him.

After praying to His Heavenly Father, those three powerful words ring out:

"LAZARUS, COME FORTH!"

It's difficult to imagine what Lazarus must have felt after having died, being placed in a tomb for three days and then, miraculously, life flooding back into his once silenced body.

Forgotten was Lazarus' discouragement and disappointment. Forgotten were those last moments when Lazarus realized that he was leaving this world.

In their places, Lazarus must have felt such joy and peace that can only come to a person when Jesus has performed a miracle in his/her life. Most assuredly, from that day forward, the lives of Lazarus and his two sisters were never the same.

When we find ourselves in a situation where it seems all hope is gone, and it's too late for a miracle, may we recall the story of Lazarus. May we be reminded that regardless of our needs, Jesus has the power over everything in our lives. May we remember that He is on the throne, He is in control, and He will arrive on the scene at just the right time.

SEEING JESUS

There are several accounts in the Bible where we read about Jesus healing the blind. One instance of the blind regaining their sight is found in Matthew 9:27-31, where it tells us the story of two blind men who were determined to be healed. When Jesus passes by, they call out to Him, asking Him to have mercy on them. Interestingly, we find Jesus walking right past them and into a house, almost like He was ignoring them.

Did His actions discourage these two blind men?

Did they just shrug their shoulders in disgust and say, "Oh well, I guess He didn't hear us. Let's just leave. He's not going to heal us"? Of course not!

The Bible tells us that these men were persistent. Having the faith that He could heal them, they were undeterred and followed Jesus into the house.

Finding Jesus, these two men are asked by Jesus if they *really* believe He is able to heal them, to which they simply reply, "Yes, Lord." As Jesus touches their eyes and tells them, *"According to your faith will it be done to you"* (Matthew 9:29), these two men miraculously received their sight. Their lives were immediately changed as their bodies received healing. It is safe to say that these men were never the same.

This is such a simple, yet beautiful, story of trusting God to meet our needs, even when obstacles get in our way. These two men were physically blind and could not see; yet their spiritual sight, which allowed them to see Jesus with their hearts, was 20/20. It was perfect and right on target.

These two formerly blind men teach us an important truth: seeing with your eyes does not mean that you are seeing with your heart.

What about us?

Do we, who are blessed with vision, fail to see Jesus with our hearts? When our needs aren't immediately supplied, do we shrug our shoulders, give up on God's ability to meet us at the point of our needs and simply walk away? Or do we persist, like these two blind men, until our needs are met?

May God open the eyes of our hearts to see Him and know Him for who He really is. May we have the persistence of the two blind men who really saw and knew who Jesus was.

May this biblical account remind us that "believing is seeing", regardless of whether it is with your eyes or with your heart.

BLIND TRUST

One of the best-known accounts of Jesus healing the blind is found in the Gospel of John 9:1-34. Here, we meet a man who was blind from birth: never saw his family or friends; never saw the beauty of leaves in the fall, or new growth of the grass and flowers in the spring; never saw the vibrant colors of a rainbow in the sky. No light.

Nothing but darkness.

Interestingly, the culture of that time held the belief that suffering, such as blindness, was caused by sin in one's life. In keeping with that tradition, when Jesus and His followers encounter the blind man, the disciples ask Jesus if this man's blindness was caused by sin in his life or by sin in his parents' lives.

Jesus' response is amazing.

Jesus replies that this man's infirmity is not a result of sin, but rather an opportunity for God to be glorified. Beautiful answer! Then Jesus reminds His disciples that He is the **_light of the world_**. Isn't it ironic that Jesus utters these words when getting ready to heal someone who has *never* seen light before?

What happens next is equally surprising.

We are told that Jesus spits on the ground and makes some mud. He anoints the eyes of the blind man with this saliva-and-dirt mixture. Jesus then instructs the man to go and wash his eyes in the Pool of Siloam. Trusting Jesus, the blind man follows these instructions, and we learn that his blind eyes are immediately healed and he goes home. There is no way this once-blind man could ever be the same. His life would certainly never be the same again.

If you're like me, you've probably heard this story and read this account many times, but have you ever pictured if *you* were that blind man?

How many of us would "blindly" (no pun intended) allow someone we've never met to put some dirt, mixed with saliva, anywhere on our faces, let alone our eyes, and not question what kind of crazy person this was?

"What in the world are you doing, Jesus? How disgusting!"

Taken a step further, how many of us would push Jesus away when He approaches us and run the other direction as fast as we can, refusing to do what He tells us to do?

Yet, isn't that what we do when we refuse to trust Jesus?

May our faith and trust in God continue to increase. As He speaks to us, may we learn to listen to His voice and trust Him without question; and may we remember that He loves us unconditionally, and that He alone knows what is best for us.

BLIND TRUST, PART 2

Skeptics.

They're all around us.

As the blind man returns home, his neighbors recognize him asking, "Isn't this the same man who used to sit and beg?" (John 9:8) There were mixed reactions, as some claimed that he *was* the same man while others said he only *looked* like him. This man, most likely becoming irritated and wanting to silence this rabble, then claims, "I *am* the man" (John 9:9).

Yet this skeptical and unconvinced mob questions him about how his eyes were opened. He recounts the story of Jesus putting mud on his eyes, telling him to wash and then miraculously, as he followed Jesus' instructions, he was able to see.

The story could have easily ended here, but it doesn't.

We find the crowd bringing this man, who was formerly blind, to the Pharisees and the Pharisees also asking him to explain how he was healed. At this point in the story, if it were us, I'm sure most of us would probably be getting quite exasperated with this situation: got to tell the story *again*; going to get everyone all stirred up *again* as I share my story; I'm not sure I want to journey down that controversial road.

He obliges the Pharisees and shares with them his story of healing. Surprisingly, we find the Pharisees divided on whether or not this man was *really* healed, especially in light of the fact that it occurred on the Sabbath. For in keeping with the customs of that day, it was considered to be sin to "work" on the Sabbath.

Just like the man's neighbors, the Pharisees were not convinced that this man is telling the truth and whether or not he really was healed, so they went to the next level: the man's parents. If *anyone* would know if this man had been blind from birth, but now could see, it would surely be his parents, right?

At this point in the story, I feel like cheering, All right! *Finally* someone will speak up and testify of the healing power of Jesus!

In my own life, I have been blessed with two precious daughters of whom I love and am equally proud of them both. I can't even begin to imagine how I would feel if either one of them were born blind. Yet, I know, without a doubt, how I would feel and react if either of my daughters was born blind; and then, at some point in their adult lives, God miraculously healed their blindness. Words couldn't even begin to describe my joy, excitement and thankfulness for this awesome miracle. You could not stop me from praising God!

How do the parents of this man who had been blind all of his life and was suddenly, miraculously, healed react? With excitement? Joy? Praise to God?

NO!

Showing what I believe had to be little, if no, emotion, they confirm that he is their son and that he was born blind; yet they refuse to admit how he was healed. Why? The Bible says that they responded to the Pharisees this way because they were afraid of being excommunicated from the synagogue if they acknowledged that Jesus was the Messiah and had performed this miracle (John 9:22). Unbelievable.

May God help us to not only thank Him for His obvious blessings in our lives, but may He give us a holy boldness to acknowledge His miracles when they occur. May we stop worrying about political correctness and being afraid of what men will think; and may we never fail to glorify God for all He has done for us.

THE SECRET ADMIRER

The Gospel of John records several encounters that Nicodemus, who was a Pharisee and member of the powerful religious counsel known as the Sanhedrin, had with Jesus (John 3:1-21; 7:50-51; 19:39-40).

Unlike some people in the Bible who weren't afraid if others knew of their faith and trust in Jesus, we find Nicodemus initially seeking Jesus at night. Many have speculated on just why it was that Nicodemus chose night for his first encounter with Jesus. However, it makes perfect sense why such an esteemed member of Jewish society would do so. The most obvious reason, of course, is that Nicodemus would not want to jeopardize his prestigious position to be seen by anyone as he conversed with Jesus, especially not by the Pharisees. He was very concerned about what men would think.

Therefore, meeting up with Jesus, under the cover of darkness, would serve to protect his powerful standing in the community, while at the same time allowing Nicodemus to learn more about Jesus.

As Nicodemus and Jesus meet face to face, we find Nicodemus prefacing his remarks to Jesus by attempting a compliment based upon the miraculous signs and wonders that Jesus had performed. It is as if Nicodemus is trying to impress Jesus.

How does Jesus react to this feigned praise? He isn't impressed; in fact, He doesn't actually address the initial compliment made by Nicodemus at all. Instead, Jesus sees right through this feeble attempt and challenges Nicodemus with a spiritual truth.

Jesus tells Nicodemus that, *"no one can see the kingdom of God unless he is born again"* (John 3:3). As Jesus explains this key concept of salvation to Nicodemus, it is safe to say that Nicodemus left his first encounter with Jesus that night a changed man.

In fact, so strong did his faith and belief in Jesus become from this initial meeting that we later find Nicodemus boldly speaking up in Jesus' defense during a meeting of the Pharisees when they were plotting to kill Jesus. Nicodemus challenged their plans by questioning, *"Does our law condemn anyone without first hearing him to find out what he is doing?"* (John 7:51)

Even though Nicodemus did not mention Jesus by name, his question, seeking justice for Jesus who was hated by the Pharisees, undoubtedly caused suspicion among this elite group. Even though his request for justice was denied, it is obvious at this point that Nicodemus' initial encounter with Jesus was apparently a life-altering experience; one that caused him to display immense boldness in front of the powerful Sanhedrin.

The faith of Nicodemus was again on display after the crucifixion of Jesus; at that time, he joined forces with Joseph of Arimathea to ask Pilate for the body of Jesus for a proper burial (John 19:39-40). Another bold move on the part of Nicodemus; his actions spoke volumes louder than any words he had ever spoken. This encounter showed Nicodemus publicly displaying his faith and allegiance as one of Jesus' followers. He no longer cared what others might think.

Nicodemus who initially came to Jesus in darkness, both literally and spiritually, found light. He no longer hid under the secretive cloak of darkness, but boldly proclaimed his faith to those around him.

The Bible doesn't tell us whatever became of him after the death of Jesus, but it is safe to say that Nicodemus became a changed man because of these encounters. Life could never be the same again for this secret admirer of Jesus.

May this example of Nicodemus remind us that we also have been enlightened by Jesus, the Light of the World. May our lives reflect the boldness and courage to shine for Jesus, regardless of life's circumstances; and when the opportunity arises, may we be like Nicodemus, and may we unashamedly proclaim our faith to those around us.

WHATEVER IT TAKES

Imagine what your life would be like if the only way you had for making a living was to sit by the side of the road and ask people to give you money; add to that the complication that you were physically blind. It's hard for us to picture ourselves in that situation. Yet such was the predicament of Bartimaeus, a blind beggar (Mark 10:46).

The ministry of Jesus had begun. The miracles He performed had quite an impact on that region, and the crowds who followed Him from town to town were growing daily. One day, as Jesus was approaching Jericho, this blind beggar heard the commotion of a huge crowd passing by and asked someone what was going on. Upon learning that this crowd was following

Jesus of Nazareth, Bartimaeus calls out, "Jesus, Son of David, have mercy on me!" (Mark 10:47)

Obviously having heard the stories about Jesus, this man was greatly motivated.

Some within the crowd of people began rebuking Bartimaeus and telling him to be quiet. It was as if they didn't want Jesus to hear his calls for help, or to take the time to help someone in need; but instead of upsetting or intimidating this blind man, their scolding didn't even phase him. In fact, it only served to motivate him to shout even louder, "Son of David, have mercy on me!"

How quickly things can change.

Jesus has that effect on situations in our lives, doesn't He?

To the surprise of those around Him, we find Jesus stopping in His tracks and ordering Bartimaeus to be brought to Him. Then Jesus asks the blind man how He can help him.

What would YOU say if you were talking face to face with Jesus and He asked you that question? Would you have enough faith to request something that will have a lasting impact for yourself and those around you?

Unabashedly, Bartimaeus asks Jesus for his sight, and Jesus immediately restores this man's vision. Bartimaeus is told that his faith has healed him. The Gospel of Luke tells us that following his healing, Bartimaeus followed Jesus (Luke 18:42). Luke also indicates that this healing caused the crowd of people who witnessed this miracle to praise God (Luke 18:43). This miracle was performed not only for the benefit of a blind beggar, but also for God's glory. I find it interesting that this biblical account of healing involves a blind man who truly "saw" Jesus for who He really was.

What would it be like to be *that* close to Jesus, and to truly know in our hearts that He can help us with our greatest needs in life?

Just ask Bartimaeus.

Did his life change? It changed physically as well as spiritually. He was never the same again.

May God raise the level of awareness in our own lives, similar to that of this blind beggar. May we unashamedly approach the throne of God with boldness when Jesus passes by; and may God help us to do whatever it takes to reach out in faith and to trust Jesus to meet our deepest needs when the opportunity arises.

AN ATTITUDE OF GRATITUDE

Have you ever wondered what it would be like to be diagnosed with an incurable disease, such as cancer? Perhaps you or someone you know has had to deal with a serious disease or illness, and would do literally anything to be whole again.

Unfortunately, although there have been many scientific advancements over the years and many treatment options for cancer, still there is no real "cure". Patients may go in remission for years, but in many cases, the disease returns and claims the lives of its victims.

In the Gospel of Luke, we read an account of ten men who had the terminal, highly contagious disease of leprosy. As it progressed from ulcerative nodules and sores on a person's body, the end result could be paralysis, wasting of muscles, gross deformities and without treatment, eventual death.[1] Those inflicted with leprosy were required to live in quarantined colonies on the edges of towns, so as not to spread the disease to the general public.

Bottom line: there was no cure for these ten men.

Until their encounter with Jesus.

Luke 17:11-19 tells us that as Jesus was traveling to Jerusalem, He passed the border between Samaria and Galilee where the ten men resided. Maintaining a proper distance, these men called out to Jesus, asking that He *"have pity on us"*. Note that they did not specifically ask Jesus for healing, although it is obvious that is exactly what they were seeking.

Jesus called back to these ten men, instructing them to show themselves to the priests. The law in that day taught that if a leper thought the disease had gone away, he was supposed to present himself to a priest, who could declare him clean. In other words, Jesus was telling them to observe the law, as noted in the Old Testament book of Leviticus, chapter 14.

The Bible account in Luke tells us that these ten lepers obeyed the instructions of Jesus and *"as they went they were cleansed"* (Luke 17:14).

An Attitude Of Gratitude

The healing was instantaneous.

Because of their encounter with Jesus, the lives of these ten lepers would never again be the same.

No doubt as they walked down the road, they looked at one another and realized the leprosy was gone. What joy and excitement must have filled their hearts, knowing that they would once again join their families and friends, no longer condemned to die from such a horrific disease! I can just imagine them laughing, shouting and running towards town as fast as they could to present themselves to the priests. Amazing!

For one of the ten men, that was not sufficient. Yes, he had excitement. Yes, he had joy in his heart; but instead of returning to town to find a priest, this man ran the opposite direction. He returned to Jesus to express his thankfulness for being healed of leprosy (Luke 17:16).

I have often wondered what made this man different from the other nine lepers.

It was his attitude.

He had an attitude of gratitude.

May this story remind us to be grateful for all the blessings we receive daily. May we remember that all good things come from God; and like this one leper, may we never fail to express an attitude of gratitude to Jesus, our high priest.

DYING TO MEET JESUS

In Luke Chapter 7, verses 11-17, we read about a woman who had not only lost her husband, but shortly thereafter, her son also died. This was not just a stressful life event for this widow, but undoubtedly she was facing incredibly dire circumstances.

In today's world, we have plenty of resources to help us cope with the present and future when losses occur, but for this widow such was not the case. Without a husband or son to provide for her, she had no financial means of support. She had nothing to look forward to; a bleak future of destitute poverty awaited her.

It was the day of her son's funeral; probably the saddest day of her life. As Jesus and His disciples approached the city of Nain, they encountered this funeral procession of the widow's son. The Bible tells us that when Jesus saw the widow woman, His heart went out to her. Filled with compassion, Jesus said to her, *"Don't cry"* (Luke 7:13).

Over the years, I have bid farewell to family members and acquaintances who have passed away. Never once do I recall anyone telling me not to cry as I grieved my loss, but that is exactly what Jesus says to this woman.

"Don't cry."

Even if a person was trying to be helpful and had good intentions, can you even begin to imagine how shocked you would feel if someone said those words to you? How would you feel if ***Jesus*** said those words to you?

"What do you mean, *'don't cry'?* Don't you realize my _____ (mother, spouse, child, etc.) has just died? How can you say such a thing to me?"

According to the Gospel of Luke, that is not what happened.

Instead, Jesus walks up and touches the coffin. The pallbearers freeze in their tracks. Jesus has just touched what was considered, at that time, something that was unclean. Facing the coffin, Jesus then says, "Young man, I say to you, get up!" (Luke 7:14)

Immediately, this previously dead person sits up and begins to talk!

Suddenly, the widow's life was changed forever. Not only was her son now alive, but her future was filled with hope. The Bible does not tell us what happened to the widow or her son following this miracle, but one thing is certain: her life and the life of her son would never be the same after this encounter with Jesus.

Seeing this miracle changed the crowd of mourners into a group of awe-struck people who began to praise God, proclaiming that Jesus was a prophet who had come to help His people. Luke tells us this good news about Jesus spread throughout Judea and the surrounding country (Luke 7:17).

When we feel overwhelmed by life's circumstances, may we recall this story of the widow. May we remember that Jesus is with us, even in the midst of the storm; and may God remind us that in those moments when we feel there is no hope, and we are facing a bleak future, that Jesus can take life's tragedies and turn them to victories.

STAND UP FOR JESUS

Have you ever broken your leg or sprained your ankle? Not only is it painful, but it becomes an inconvenience, albeit temporary, for you and your family. What about if it was permanent, and you found yourself paralyzed?

Not able to stand up.

Not able to walk.

Ever again.

We read about such a man in the Gospel of Mark, Chapter 2:1-12. This paralyzed man had to depend on his family and friends to transport him. They would do this by picking him up on his mat and carrying him wherever he needed to go.

On one particular day, Jesus was coming home to Capernaum from a long journey. Talk of the many miracles He had performed preceded Him, and when He arrived to the house, He was welcomed by a massive crowd of people. The paralyzed man and his friends were among the multitude seeking Jesus. They believed that if they could get this man to Jesus, he would be healed.

There was one problem: the house was filled to overflow, with so many people that the doorway was blocked and there was no room for anyone else to enter the house.

No way for this man to reach Jesus.

I can just sense the frustration this man and his friends must have felt. "Let's see…there's no way we can get through the doorway…But we've carried our friend all this way, and there's no way we're giving up now."

As Jesus preached God's Word to the crowd, the paralytic and his friends were formulating a plan. They must have realized that there was more than one way to reach Jesus. They picked up the paralytic and carried him up the stairs to the roof. Upon dismantling a section of the roof, these men with a plan gently lowered their friend into the room where Jesus was. As the crowd watched this remarkable scene, Jesus, recognizing the faith of these men, healed the paralyzed man, telling him, *"Friend, your sins are forgiven"* (Mark 2:5).

The Bible tells us that hearing these words, the Pharisees and teachers began thinking to themselves that Jesus was blaspheming because only God could forgive sins. Jesus *knew* what they were thinking and rebuked these religious leaders. *"Which is easier: to say to the paralytic, 'your sins are forgiven,' or to say 'Get up, take your mat and walk?'"* Jesus then said to the paralyzed man, *"I tell you, get up, take your mat and go home"* (Mark 2:9-11). ***Immediately,*** the man who had been paralyzed stood up in front of the multitude, took up his mat and went home, praising God. The crowd was amazed and also gave praise to God for this healing miracle.

This is an incredible account of how faith can change lives.

Just ask the man who had been paralyzed.

Just four simple words: *"Thy sins be forgiven."* From that moment on, his life would never be the same again.

More important than the physical healing was the spiritual healing that took place in this man's life.

May this story show us how God can accomplish great things when we place our faith and trust in Him. May we be reminded that He has a plan for our lives. May we know, without a doubt, that with God <u>all</u> things are possible.

TOUCHING JESUS

The advancements in medicine, medical procedures and physician training have come a long way since the days of Jesus: but even with today's modern technology available to mankind, sickness and disease are still rampant.

The financial costs of today's medical care can be overwhelming, with some spending every penny they own for a cure. Sadly, sometimes families are even forced to declare bankruptcy, due to exorbitant medical expenses. Sometimes a loved one is cured by the medical community, and other times they are not.

During the ministry of Jesus, the Bible tells us that it was not unusual for crowds to follow Him wherever He went. In the Gospel of Mark, Chapter 5, we find a large crowd gathering around Jesus as He stepped off a boat by the lake. This crowd began to follow as Jesus walked along and they "pressed" around Him.

The stories told of miracles wrought through the healing hands of Jesus caused everyone to want to be near Him. This included a woman who had suffered a great deal under the care of many physicians over a twelve-year span of her life. She had literally spent *all* of her money; yet the Bible tells us that her illness continued to worsen. She, being a woman of faith, reasoned that if she could just touch the cloak of Jesus, she would be healed.

I can just picture the scene as the crowd surrounds Jesus. All of a sudden, a woman boldly and unashamedly pushes her way through, coming up behind Jesus and touching the hem of His garment. We are told that she is healed *immediately*.

Instantly.

At once.

Without delay.

She felt in her body that she was "freed from her suffering".

Jesus was also aware that someone had just received healing. He turns to the crowd pressing around Him and wants to know who touched His clothes.

I can picture the ever-practical disciples reminding Jesus that everyone seemed to be touching Him. Were it not so serious, their response to Jesus is almost comical; but He seems to ignore their remarks as He continues to gaze into the faces of the crowd.

At that moment, the woman fearful, yet excited to be healed, steps forward and shares her story with the Master Healer. As He looks into her eyes, Jesus declares to her, *"Daughter, your faith has healed you. Go in peace and be freed from your suffering"* (Mark 5:34).

As this woman discovered, her life would never be the same after her encounter with Jesus. Touching Jesus was the best decision she had ever made.

May this Bible account encourage us that we can boldly bring our physical needs to Jesus. May we reach out to Him and allow Him to touch our lives in such a way that our deepest needs are met; and may we realize that Jesus, the Master Physician, is able to heal all manners of sickness and disease when we come to Him in faith.

FALLING AT THE FEET OF JESUS

As parents, we love our children and would do virtually anything we could to help them when they are in need.

Try to imagine how it would feel if one of your children was dying. You've consulted with the best physicians, taken him/her to the finest medical facilities, had the latest tests run and given him/her the best medications available. All of it is of no avail; your child is quickly spiraling towards eternity.

Being a mother of two, I totally understand how devastated I would feel if one of my daughters was on her deathbed. I know I would pray and seek God's face for her healing. I would also contact everyone I knew via telephone, Facebook and any other available means, and ask people to join along with me seeking divine intervention.

In the Gospel of Luke, Chapter 8, we find Jairus, a ruler of the synagogue, facing this situation. His only daughter, a girl of about twelve years of age, was dying.

Obviously Jairus didn't have the many avenues of social media, and he didn't have all the advances in modern medicine that we do today, but he did have faith. He believed in the power of prayer, and for this, he physically sought the face of Jesus.

The Bible tells us that Jairus reached out to Jesus and literally "fell at Jesus' feet", ***pleading*** with Jesus to come to his house. This father with great faith asked Jesus to put His hands upon his daughter and she would live.

As Jesus and His disciples were walking, someone from his home approached Jairus and broke the news that his daughter was dead, and suggested, *"Don't bother the teacher anymore"* (Luke 8:49). Surely, at this point, Jairus must have been overwhelmed with grief and full of despair. He had lost all hope for a miracle. His only daughter was dead, but at the lowest point in the life of this father, Jesus said to Jairus, *"Don't be afraid; just believe, and she will be healed"* (Luke 9:50).

Continuing on to the home of Jairus, we find mourners crying loudly. Jesus rebukes the crowd, telling them to stop wailing as the girl is *"not dead but asleep"* (Luke 9:52). The unbelieving crowd laughs at Jesus' remarks, because they *know* that she is dead.

As Jesus walks into this home with Peter, John, James and the girl's parents, they enter the girl's room. Taking her by the hand, Jesus commands the young girl to get up. Immediately, she stands up as if nothing was wrong.

Wait, that's not all. Jesus then does another surprising thing. He instructs the girl's parents to give her something to eat, reflecting a glimpse into the humanity of Jesus. The girl must be hungry! The fact that Jesus has to remind the parents of this young girl's basic need for food is such a commentary on how awestruck and astonished her parents must have been at this point. They've just seen their daughter raised from the dead and are seemingly clueless what to do next.

Through this encounter with Jesus, the life of this twelve-year-old girl was restored. She and her parents would never be the same again.

Having read this biblical account over the years, I have always thought of it as just another story of Jesus' miracles; but as I sit here today and ponder its significance to me on a more personal level, how would I react at this point? Besides the obvious grief and devastation of losing a child, would I have the faith of Jairus? Or, would I begin making funeral arrangements? It's quite easy to take the high road and say I would trust Jesus, but quite different when I attempt to personalize this extraordinary account of healing within my own family circle.

As we go through our daily lives, may this biblical account serve to remind us that regardless of the intense grief we may be experiencing to never abandon hope. May we be reminded daily of just how precious our children are; and may our faith and hope be a reflection of Jesus' words to Jairus: *"Don't be afraid; just believe."*

DEATH SENTENCE

It started out as many other mornings; Jesus again appeared in the temple courts where "all the people" gathered around Him. As He sat down and prepared to teach these hungry souls about the goodness of God, He is suddenly interrupted as another crowd enters the temple area.

Made up of the Pharisees and teachers of the law, this noisy crowd is different. Their purpose: to confront Jesus in an attempt to trap Him, but Jesus is one step ahead of them. He knows what they are up to, and He is about to use this moment as the **ultimate** object lesson.

As the narrative continues, we learn that these religious leaders had brought with them a woman caught in adultery (John 8:3). The men question Jesus regarding the Law of Moses, reminding Him that in the Law,

Moses commanded them to stone such women. They ask Jesus what He thinks should be done.

It's interesting to note that even though these men were citing the "Law of Moses", it was only a partial truth. In both of the Old Testament passages of Leviticus 20:10 and Deuteronomy 22:22, we find that the Law required both the man and woman caught in adultery to be stoned; yet they only sought punishment for the woman. Where was the man? We are not told anything at all about the other half of the guilty couple, and apparently they are not seeking any degree of punishment for him.

At this point, it would have been so easy for Jesus to turn around and rebuke these men for misquoting the Law; but that's not how this story unfolds.

As we read further, we see Jesus react to these men with a very strange response. Instead of verbally responding, He bends down and begins writing on the ground with His finger.

I can just picture the religious leaders watching Jesus with curiosity, looking at one another with quizzical looks on their faces, scratching their beards and shaking their heads in confused disbelief.

Death Sentence

They have all gathered around this woman, rocks in their hands, anxious to carry out her death sentence. I imagine they are staring at her with such hatred in their hearts and indignant contempt in their eyes. After all, she is a *sinner,* and she **must be punished** for her indiscretions.

Determined to get a response from Jesus, they incessantly persist. They demand an answer, and they're about to get one. Jesus floors them as He stands up, looking each one of the religious leaders in the eyes and announces, *"If any one of you is without sin, let him be the first to throw a stone at her"* (John 8:7).

This is definitely not the answer they were anticipating.

Within that holier-than-thou crowd of religious leaders, *no one* could boast of being without sin.

Suddenly, the thrill and excitement of punishing this "sinner" woman evaporated into thin air: gone; vanished; erased from existence.

Jesus stoops down and once again writes on the ground with His finger. The religious leaders are now filled with frustration, as they realize their scheme to trap Jesus has failed.

One by one, as the only sound heard is the "thud" as they drop their rocks on the ground, we find the angry rabble walking away; the older ones first, followed by the younger ones, until no one is left except Jesus and the woman. Jesus asks her where everyone had gone. *"Has no one condemned you?"* (John 8:10). When she responds that no one does, Jesus tells her that He does not condemn her either. He commands her to leave her life of sin.

What has just happened?

Can you even begin to imagine how the woman must have felt?

One minute she stood there terrified, facing a certain death sentence for committing such a horrible sin. The next moment she is pardoned by Jesus, the *only one* standing there without sin; the only one who had a right to condemn her to death.

Yet, He casts no stone.

Instead, He bestows forgiveness.

Jesus quite literally **saved her life;** a life that would never be the same again.

Sound familiar?

This biblical narrative reminds us that without Jesus' forgiveness, we are all like the woman in this story. Without Jesus in our lives, we are guilty of sin and face certain death, doomed to the prospect of no hope and eternal separation from God. Romans 3:23 reminds us that *"We have all sinned and fallen short of God's glory."*

We may be quick to judge the religious leaders, but our own sinful natures are no better than theirs. Matthew 7:3 says so aptly: *"Why do you look at the speck of sawdust in your brother's eye and pay no attention to the plank in your own eye?"*

May this biblical account in John 8:1-11 serve to remind us that our focus should not be on the transgressions of others, but upon the need for forgiveness in our own lives. May God grant us the wisdom to drop our rocks of condemnation towards others; and may He help us to walk away from sin, and seek Him above all else.

DON'T LOSE HOPE

When you think of a person who is referred to as an "invalid", what is the first thing that pops into your mind? Someone who is handicapped, sickly or incurable, right? Someone who cannot manage on his/her own; someone who depends on others to make it through life?

Such was the man we read about in the Gospel of John, Chapter 5. Although we are not told how old he is, it is obvious that he has, in fact, been an invalid for thirty-eight years. Think about it, nearly four decades. In this narrative, we find him, along with other unfortunate members of the community, among them the lame, the blind and the paralyzed in Jerusalem, lying near a pool known as Bethesda.

Why were these people there?

As we read further, we learn that these individuals were lying near the pool, waiting for something to happen. The Bible tells us, *"From time to time an angel of the Lord would come down and stir up the waters. The first one into the pool after each such disturbance would be cured of whatever disease he had"* (John 5:3-4).

Jesus approaches this particular man who had been an invalid for so many years, and asks the man a very basic question: *"Do you want to get well?"* (John 5:6).

For those of us on the outside looking in, you would think this question would elicit a simple answer: "Of course I want to be healed!"

It seems like a no-brainer, right?

That's not how the man responds. Rather than giving Jesus an emphatic "Yes, I would **love** to be healed", the man's response reflects his seemingly hopeless condition. After being in such poor health for so many years, he is basically discouraged and downtrodden. He has accepted his lot in life and has given up hope of being healed or of ever living a normal life. Instead of expressing a heartfelt desire to be whole again, this paralyzed man simply explains to Jesus **why** he has never been healed.

Understanding this man's discouraged, hopeless spirit, and knowing that the man's deepest desire was to be healed, Jesus says to him, *"Get up! Pick up your mat and walk"* (John 5:8). The Bible tells us that the man was immediately cured and did as Jesus commanded: he picked up his mat and walked.

What a life-changing experience this was for the man!

He is healed.

He can walk.

A man whose life situation seemed hopeless was now filled with hope again.

His encounter with Jesus left him a changed man.

He was most definitely never the same.

This story makes me wonder: have you ever been there?

Perhaps you're not physically paralyzed like this man in the Gospel of John, but when life's tribulations and trials come your way, are you emotionally or spiritually paralyzed? Do you find yourself making excuses and trying to figure things out on your own, rather than looking to Jesus Christ for the solution?

May this story remind us that when things look hopeless and we feel discouraged, Jesus stands next to us, ready and willing to meet us at the point of our greatest need.

Be encouraged. Don't lose hope.

"May the God of hope fill you with all joy and peace as you trust in him, so that you may overflow with hope by the power of the Holy Spirit" (Romans 15:13).

MORE THAN ENOUGH

During His brief lifetime on earth, Jesus performed so many miracles of healing, both physical and spiritual, that I think we sometimes forget that He was human and had the same basic needs that we have. He got tired; He got hungry and thirsty; He became discouraged, and even sad at times.

After Jesus received news of the death of John the Baptist, He went by boat with the disciples to a quiet place away from the crowds to get some rest; but the Bible tells us that *"many who saw them leaving recognized them and ran on foot from all the towns and got there ahead of them"* (Mark 6:32-33).

The boat lands on the shore and Jesus sees the massive crowd awaiting His arrival. He feels deep compassion for these people and begins ministering to their needs, healing their bodies and teaching them the truths of God.

As the day goes on, some of the disciples approach Jesus to remind Him of the lateness of the hour and the fact that this crowd must be hungry. They suggest that Jesus disband the group of people so they can go to town and buy themselves some food.

The disciples wait for Jesus to respond, but the answer is not what they are expecting. Jesus says, *"They do not need to go away. You give them something to eat"* (Matt. 14:16).

I can just picture the disciples looking at Jesus, looking at one another, and then mumbling amongst themselves. "What does he mean? How are <u>we</u> going to feed **so many** people? It would take over half a year's wages to feed this crowd!"

At this point, one of the disciples, Andrew the brother of Simon Peter, breaks the silence, advising them that there is a boy in the crowd who has five small barley loaves and two small fish, but *"how far will they go among so many?"* (John 6:8-9). In the eyes of the disciples, there appears to be no solution to this dilemma.

The disciples <u>forget</u> who Jesus is. Yes, He's human; yes, He gets hungry just like them, but Jesus is also the Son of God. If He can heal the sick, raise the dead, cleanse the lepers and cause the blind to see, He is just as able to feed this enormous crowd of five thousand (not counting women and children).

Jesus instructs the disciples to bring this meager fare to Him and to have all the people sit down in groups. He then gives thanks to God for the five loaves and two fishes, blesses it, breaks it and has the disciples distribute it among the crowd.

Talk about the ultimate "dinner on the grounds!" Not only are we told that everyone in the crowd was fed, but somehow there are twelve baskets full of leftovers! This is definitely one for the record books.

Although the Bible doesn't indicate that anyone being fed realized what an incredible miracle had just occurred, I can just imagine the young boy who gave all he had to Jesus, beaming with pride for his donation to the cause. For what originally appeared to be insufficient for the need became "more than enough" with Jesus entered the equation.

What lesson can we glean from this encounter with Jesus? May we not be hesitant to offer our gifts to Jesus. May we realize that little is **much** when God is in it; and may we be reminded that regardless of the size and scope of our offering, when we place it in the hands of Jesus, He can take it, use it for God's glory and make it more than enough to bless those around us.

SAVING THE BEST FOR LAST

One of the most precious experiences in our lives is when we witness two people pledging their hearts and lives to one another.

I'm talking about weddings, of course. We've all attended them and taken part in these festive occasions. The Bible tells us in Genesis 2:24 that this is God's plan for us: *"For this reason a man will leave his father and mother and be united to his wife, and they will become one flesh."*

Weddings don't just "happen".

Weddings take a lot of work, planning and can be very costly. You want everything to be "just right", and you want your guests to be well taken care of on that special day.

In the American culture, weddings are a one-day event, but depending on the culture, the length of the wedding day may be celebrated very differently. For instance, in the country of Israel in the days of Jesus, weddings were usually celebrated for an entire week. They entailed cultural festivities, but ultimately featured the basic staples of most weddings: food and drink. Entire communities would come together to celebrate with the happy couple. It was understood that everyone was invited, and to not attend was considered quite rude.

In the Gospel of John, verses 2-11, we read about a wedding that Jesus, His mother, Mary, and His disciples attended. During the height of this celebration, the unthinkable occurred--they ran out of wine. In today's world, no big deal; you would just run down to the corner liquor store and buy what you needed, but it wasn't quite so simple back in that day and time.

Taking a closer look at that culture helps us understand why this appeared to be such a huge problem. Because wine played such a central part in the wedding hospitality, running out of wine would equate to showing disrespect to your guests. An event that was so vibrant and joyful one moment could quite literally turn ugly in a flash.

In this particular Bible narrative, Mary advised Jesus about the wine dilemma, believing that he would have a solution. While we do not know if Mary thought her son could solve this problem practically or supernaturally, it is clear that she placed her trust in Him to resolve the ordeal. In fact, so confident is Mary that Jesus holds the answer to this dilemma that she commands the servants to *"Do whatever he tells you"* (John 2:5).

Obediently, and without questioning Jesus' instructions, these servants fill six large, stone water jars with water and take a sample of the water to the master of the banquet.

It is no longer water.

It has suddenly, and miraculously, become wine.

The problem is solved, and the first miracle of Jesus has just occurred. We are told that because of this turning water into wine, Jesus *"revealed his glory and his disciples put their faith in him"* (John 2:11). This event changed their perception of Jesus and revealed who He truly was. The disciples, henceforth, could never be the same.

You would think the master of the banquet would be thrilled with the provision of more wine for the guests, and a crisis averted; but instead of being grateful, we find him expressing disdain to the bridegroom that he saved the best wine for last.

What about us?

Can we see ourselves in this biblical narrative? Who do we most resemble?

Are we like the master of the banquet, forgetting how God meets our needs and failing to express our gratitude in those times?

Are we like the servants, who unreservedly obeyed Jesus' instructions?

Are we like the disciples, who placed their trust in Jesus as they witnessed Him performing His first miracle?

Or, are we like Mary, the mother of Jesus, who came to Him with a problem, submitted to His authority and trusted Him implicitly to solve the problem?

I think that perhaps there's a little bit of each of these people within us.

Instead of failing to express our gratitude to the Lord for His many provisions and countless blessings in our lives, like the master of the banquet, may we truly be thankful for all we've been given.

May we be like the servants, obeying God without reservation.

May we be like the disciples, placing our trust in Jesus as we witness the daily miracles in our lives.

May we be like Mary, coming to Jesus with our problems, trusting and believing that He has the solution.

May this scripture passage inspire and encourage us to give our all to Jesus, from this day forward, and to not "save the best for last".

NO ORDINARY DAY

For those of us in the Monday-Friday working world, we find that many of our days are spent doing repetitive, and sometimes mundane, tasks over and over again. Even though I'm a legal secretary, most of my days are filled with challenging opportunities that can come up when you least expect it; definitely not mundane. In fact, I often joke that I'm in the wrong profession. I should have joined the local fire department, as I find myself putting out fires on a daily basis.

It's not a laughing matter to those who serve in law enforcement and fire-rescue occupations. Their jobs, quite dangerous and many times life-threatening, are anything but ordinary.

In the days of Jesus, the keeping of law and order, which included witnessing the punishment and subsequent deaths of convicted criminals, was undoubtedly a routine job responsibility of the Roman centurion officer and his entourage. Crucifixion was a common punishment for those who broke the law, so much so that most guards probably took it in stride and didn't think twice about those executions.

Who can even begin to fathom what went on in the thoughts of the Roman centurion, as he witnessed the beating and took part in the crucifixion of Jesus Christ? Perhaps he sensed something was different about this particular man who was literally beaten within an inch of his life.

True, the security detail was heavier than normal. True, this man Jesus seemed to have an unusually large crowd following Him. As he looked around, this centurion officer must have seen the different reactions of the crowd. Some seemed full of anger and hatred to the point of making fun of Jesus. There were others weeping and those who appeared truly heartbroken as they watched Jesus, whom they believed was an innocent man, suffering a horrendous and agonizing death on the cross between two common criminals.

As Jesus took His final breath with a loud cry, the day suddenly became anything but ordinary. In Matthew 27:51-53, the Bible says, *"At that moment the curtain of the temple was torn in two from top to bottom. The earth shook and the rocks split. The tombs broke open and the bodies of many holy people who had died were raised to life. They came out of the tombs, and after Jesus' resurrection they went into the holy city and appeared to many people."*

At this point, it is interesting to compare the Gospels of Matthew and Luke as we gauge the reaction of the Roman centurion. Matthew 27:54 tells us that when the centurion, and those with him who were guarding Jesus, saw the earthquake and all that had happened, they were terrified and exclaimed, *"Surely he was the Son of God!"* Luke 23:47 goes a step further, stating, *"The centurion, seeing what had happened, praised God and said, 'Surely this was a righteous man.'"*

While we can only speculate whatever became of this Roman centurion, I'm of the opinion that once he experienced firsthand the unusual phenomena that occurred upon the death of Jesus, his life could never be the same again. Because of that, perhaps at some point in his life, he became a believer of Jesus. Perhaps he became a very vocal witness for the Lord, sharing all that he had seen and heard with those around him.

This had been no ordinary day in the life of the centurion.

May this story challenge us to look at our daily circumstances with fresh insight. May we realize that every day we live is a gift from God, and that no day is "ordinary" when Jesus Christ is your Lord and Savior.

A CONGREGATION OF TWO

We've all been there.

You start out optimistic and things in your life appear to be going incredibly well.

Then it happens.

Someone or something in your life lets you down. Disappointment and discouragement move in with a vengeance, replacing all possible hope of overcoming this latest adversity.

Yet, putting things into perspective, when I consider some of life's setbacks and disappointments, they seem so trivial compared to the grief and shock experienced by the disciples after the death of Jesus.

I cannot even begin to fathom how the followers of Jesus must have felt after witnessing His brutal beating, crucifixion and subsequent death: overwhelming grief;

unbearable sadness; all hope abandoned and future plans dashed to the ground. Where do we go from here? How do we cope? What do we do now?

As they journeyed on the road to Emmaus, we find two such followers of Jesus discussing the unbelievable events that had transpired within the past few days. Then suddenly, Jesus appears and begins walking with the two, but somehow they don't recognize Him. How is that possible?

Perhaps it is because they watched Him die on the cross and are not anticipating meeting up with a walking, talking, living Jesus. Or perhaps, as Luke 24:17 says, *"Their faces were downcast"*, and they are so grief-stricken and heartbroken that they don't look directly into the face of this stranger who has joined them.

Jesus inquires what the two are discussing, and it is at the point that one of the followers, Cleopas, perceives that Jesus must be a visitor to Jerusalem because He doesn't seem to know about the recent events that have taken place.

As Jesus presses them to explain, they detail the life and ministry of Jesus of Nazareth. In Luke 24:20-21, they share, *"The chief priests and our rulers handed him over to be sentenced to death, and they crucified him; but we had hoped that he was the one who was going to redeem Israel."*

Listening to their accounts, Jesus rebukes them for their inability to believe the words of the prophets, who foretold that Christ would suffer and subsequently enter glory. We find Jesus preaching an unforgettable sermon to this congregation of two, explaining what the Scriptures said concerning Him. What a message that must have been!

As evening approaches, the two followers convince Jesus to stay with them, but it is not until they are seated at the table and Jesus blesses the bread, breaks it and serves it to the two men that *"their eyes were opened and they recognized him"* (Luke 24:31).

Then, just as suddenly as He arrives, Jesus disappears from their sight. The two men were so thrilled with this encounter with Jesus that they immediately returned to Jerusalem to share this miraculous experience with the apostles.

While the Bible doesn't tell us anything further about these two followers of Jesus, it is safe to assume that this encounter with the resurrected Christ was life-changing for both of them. What a testimony this must have given them to share with others. They would never be the same after this experience.

I've often wondered why the followers of Jesus didn't understand the Old Testament prophecies, didn't comprehend His mission and didn't recognize who Jesus really was. Perhaps it's like the saying, "You can't see the forest for the trees." Perhaps it was impossible for them to realize how the Scriptures were being fulfilled, because they were standing so close to the situation.

What can we learn from this passage?

May we be encouraged, like the two followers of Jesus, that when we personally encounter Him, our eyes will be opened to His love and forgiveness. May we especially recall the reality of His resurrection during those times when we feel downtrodden and discouraged. May the resurrection of Jesus become so real to us that we can't wait to share it with others.

PART II

"SOMEBODY CALL 9-1-1!"

The toddler grew increasingly restless in the high chair as she sat near her mother, who was busy typing a doctoral dissertation on the old black manual typewriter at the kitchen table.

Squirming around in the high chair, the child finally wriggled loose from her seated position and managed to stand up. Quickly rising to catch her daughter, all good intentions failed as the high chair toppled backward, spilling its precious cargo onto the floor with a loud *CRASH!*

Standing there in disbelief and scooping up her baby, the mother began calling desperately for her husband, *"Herb, come quickly!"* As she gazed upon the lifeless body she now held in her arms, she immediately realized the baby was not breathing. *"Herb, I need your* *help **NOW***" she screamed, but her heroic cries for help remained unanswered.

Praying a silent prayer for direction, God spoke to the child's mother and inspired her to perform CPR. Gently placing her mouth over the baby's blue lips, she began blowing her own breath into the child's mouth. Minutes seemed like hours to this frightened mother, as she poured the gift of life into her baby. Suddenly, miraculously, the baby began to cry.

The year was 1959, and I was that baby.

My mother had never heard of CPR, and there was no such thing as placing an emergency telephone call to 9-1-1; yet somehow she knew **exactly** what to do.

My mother didn't call 9-1-1 on that fateful day in 1959.

Instead, God came on the scene and answered the cries of a desperate mother.

As my mother related this story years later, it was obvious that God had other plans for me. One of my favorite scripture verses is Jeremiah 29:11: *"For I know the plans I have for you," declares the Lord, "plans to prosper you and not to harm you, plans to give you hope and a future."*

Ever since the first time I heard my mother tell me the story of my highchair accident, I have firmly believed that God raised me up for a purpose.

Please allow me to share with you, in the final chapters of this book, some of the life-changing encounters with Jesus Christ that I have experienced:

Encounters that rendered me never the same.

THE WAITING GAME

The winter weather had been mild for December in the Northern Virginia suburbs, yet there was no denying that Christmas was in the air. My best friend Jean and I were excited to be a part of the youth choir of our church Christmas program. We had attended every rehearsal and knew each song by heart. Our parents seemed to share in our excitement, as they took turns dropping us off at rehearsals every week.

On this particular evening, when the rehearsal was over, we walked to the designated agreed-upon meeting place, but no one was there to pick us up. After waiting several minutes, we began searching the entire parking lot but to no avail. Our parents were nowhere to be found. We soon realized that we did not have a way to get home. As the parking lot emptied, and we stood in the chilly night air, Jean and I agreed that we should start walking home. After all, we only lived four blocks away, which was no big deal for a couple of fourth-graders.

Growing up, our respective parents had taught both of us to use caution and to look both ways before crossing the street. In front of us loomed a major highway, yet we felt prepared to handle it. We just needed to watch for cars coming down the road and then to proceed when the way was clear. As we began running across the intersection, Jean was ahead of me when suddenly I heard the loud squeal of a car's brakes. As I watched in disbelief, I saw her body knocked across the roadway and heard the sickening thud as she hit the pavement.

How could we have been so careless? Why did we not see the vehicle coming toward us? Even though it was very dark outside, the driver had apparently neglected to turn on his headlights and was virtually invisible to us as we raced across the highway.

An ambulance finally arrived and whisked Jean to the hospital. Fortunate to not have been killed by the racing vehicle, Jean suffered many cuts, bruises and a shattered anklebone. Even though people told me that

I was the "lucky" one, I often wondered why it was her and not I who was struck down by a car.

Although it was a mutual decision to walk home instead of waiting for our parents, the guilt hung over me as I relived the emotional trauma of watching my best friend hit by a careless driver. Our hasty decision to veer from what we knew was right cost Jean dearly. We would later find out that both sets of parents thought the other set was supposed to pick us up, and as a result neither of them arrived at the designated time. The accident happened because two children grew tired of waiting for their parents, became impatient and decided to take matters into their own hands.

This particular incident reminds me that as children of God, we tend to grow impatient with Him. We can't understand why it seems so long for God to answer our prayers. Somehow we forget that He sees the big picture, knows what is best for us and will bring the right answer in His perfect timing. We lack the faith to trust Him with our concerns and problems; instead of patiently waiting for Him, we prefer to take matters into our own hands. Forgetting that He is sovereign, we think we can solve our problems by ourselves without His help.

We need to refocus our trust in God, because as we read in Isaiah 30:18, *"Blessed are all who wait for Him!"*

May the Lord teach us to wait patiently upon Him in our time of need. When we are tempted to proceed without Him, even though we know we should wait, may we be reminded that He has our best interests at heart and He will arrive at the right time.

WHAT A FRIEND

I was brought up as a Roman Catholic and through my growing-up years participated in the sacraments of the church, which included baptism as an infant, confession, communion and confirmation. While I attended church weekly with my family, which Catholics describe as being a "good" Catholic, as I became a teenager I sensed that there was something missing in my life. I can recall after going to confession, telling my sins to the parish priest, and reciting penance for the sins that I had committed, how I never really felt a sense of being forgiven.

The turning point in my life occurred back in 1973 when I was invited to attend a crusade at the Melbourne Civic Auditorium. I had no idea what a "crusade" was, nor why it was such a big deal, but I was curious enough to find out more. As I entered the auditorium, there seemed to be electricity in the air. Shortly after finding a seat in the bleachers, upbeat music began to play. Some people were clapping to the music, some people were singing and some people were raising their hands. Before long, I found myself also clapping along with the music.

Then the speaker for the evening was introduced. He spoke about how we all look for peace and happiness in our lives but can't seem to find it. He said that each of us was born into a world of sin, and how this sin condemned us to spend an eternity without hope. Then he explained that so great was God's love for us that He had sent His son, Jesus Christ, to take all of our bad deeds, our "sins", upon Himself by dying a cruel death on a wooden cross, as a sacrifice for our sins, so that we might have the gift of eternal life with God.

I sat there and listened as the speaker explained how people look for happiness and satisfaction in their lives through school, friends or work, but never quite seem to find it. I suddenly realized he was describing my life.

As he spoke passionately about the birth, death and resurrection of Jesus Christ, it suddenly began to make sense to me. The peace I had been searching for all of my life could only be found through salvation in Jesus Christ! We now had a choice to make. Each of us held the key to our destiny, and it was up to us to make that decision. We could seek God's forgiveness for our sins and accept His gift of eternal life, or we could reject this gift and be condemned to an eternity without God.

When the speaker asked if anyone in the audience would like to receive Jesus as his/her personal savior, my heart was pounding so loud I thought everyone around me could hear it. I got up out of my seat and quickly made my way down the aisle to the front of the auditorium, along with dozens of other people. As they began praying for me, I also joined in, asking Jesus to forgive me for my sinful life and to be my Lord and Savior. For the first time in my life, I recall feeling that *"peace that transcends all understanding"* (Philippians 4:7) enter my heart. The emptiness and unhappiness I'd been experiencing for years suddenly melted away.

I had entered that auditorium feeling miserable, all alone, and that no one really cared about me. On that night, Jesus came into my heart and became my *"friend who sticks closer than a brother"* (Prov. 18:24).

The Bible tells us, *"For it is by grace you have been saved, through faith—and this is not from yourselves, it is the gift of God—not by works, so that no one can boast"* (Eph. 2:8).

Accepting Jesus Christ as my personal Savior was the most important decision I have ever made. Since that night in 1973, He's been with me through the valleys as well as the mountaintops of my life. He's been my constant comfort in troubled times and my greatest cheerleader in moments of victory.

Life for me has never been the same.

If you're reading this book and have never asked Jesus Christ to become your Lord and Savior, what is stopping you from accepting His amazing grace?

TESTIMONY OF HEALING

Isn't it strange how a day can start out one way, but somehow before the day is over, it has turned your life totally upside down? Such was the predicament I found myself in when I was twenty-two years old.

It was the spring of 1980. I woke up that morning feeling fine, but as the day wore on, I experienced a continual, crushing pain in my left chest. The pain seemed to increase with each breath I took. My husband took me to the emergency room of a local hospital, where they immediately ran an EKG to assess whether or not I was having a heart attack. Somehow I knew it was not my heart, and the test results confirmed this.

A pain-relieving medication was injected into my left chest wall and the sharp pain gradually subsided. A month later the sharp pain returned, now accompanied by an irritating cough. X-rays were ordered revealing a "mass" in my left lung. The doctors initially diagnosed me with a possible case of tuberculosis and antibiotics were prescribed to combat it. When my TB test results came back negative, a new set of X-rays ordered two weeks later revealed that this mass was growing at an alarming rate.

At this point I was sent to a lung specialist, who meticulously reviewed my X-rays and medical records. He told us that I might need surgery to remove this mass, which was quite possibly a tumor, but he stated that because of my young age and other factors, there was only about a five percent chance that it was a tumor. My mind did not register the "five percent" part of his diagnosis, but only the word "tumor".

Returning to the doctor a few days later, I underwent a bronchoscopy to allow the doctor to see what this mass actually was; the doctor's diagnosis of a tumor was confirmed. He tried to biopsy it for further analysis, but when the tumor began to bleed, he was unable to do so for fear of possible hemorrhage. The lung specialist then advised us that I would need surgery to remove this tumor. The upper lobe of my left lung would have to be removed as well.

On the night before my scheduled surgery, another chest X-ray was taken. Because many churches and individuals had been praying for me, I was anticipating God's healing and no need for surgery. However, the final report revealed that the tumor, still present, was even larger than the last set of X-rays. We were all shocked beyond words.

On the morning of September 2, 1980, I was taken to the operating room for surgery, which was supposed to take three to four hours to complete. So when the surgeon came out of the operating room an hour and a half later to talk with my family, they thought he was coming out to tell them good news. Instead, the surgeon stated that the circumstances were "worse than we initially thought". Because of the location of the tumor and other complicated factors, it was necessary to remove not only the tumor, but my ***entire left lung***.

I recall waking up from the anesthesia and being presented with the news. It couldn't have really happened – it must have been just a bad dream. As I felt the set of tight bandages across my chest, the reality hit me like a ton of bricks—it was real.

As I went home from the hospital a week after my surgery, I was physically drained. I felt so depressed and bitter, believing that God had let me down. I was horribly confused why God had not healed me and why I had to endure such a devastating surgery at only twenty-two years of age. My depression deepened to the point where I even refused to go to church, using the excuse that I was recuperating and could not sit through a church service.

About two months after the surgery, I was invited to attend a revival service at a Pentecostal church. Although I protested and listed many reasons why I could not go to church, somehow I managed to get dressed and reluctantly went.

Near the end of the church service, the evangelist invited the congregation to walk through a prayer line for any special needs they may have. A woman sitting behind me tapped me on the shoulder and suggested that I should be prayed for; but my feelings of resentment towards God welled up inside of me, as I began to ponder, "Why should I get prayed for at this point?

I've already gone through surgery; what can God do for me now?"

As I continued to rationalize in my mind how ridiculous getting prayed for would be, the woman behind me persisted. She would simply not take no for an answer.

Slowly I stood up and walked down the aisle, stepping into the prayer line. As the evangelist and other ministers laid their hands upon my forehead and shoulders and began praying, something began to happen in that little church building. Someone began speaking in tongues. Another person gave this interpretation: *"I have heard your prayers and seen your tears; I will heal you"* (2 Kings 20:5). While all of this was going on, I felt an unbelievable feeling, which I can only describe like a surge of electricity immediately going through my body.

The following morning as I awoke, I no longer felt weak. It was almost as if I had never gone through the lung surgery. Six weeks later, when I returned to the lung specialist for a check-up, he was amazed at my progress. I told him I felt better with one lung than I had with two lungs. Although he cited some medical reason why that could be possible, I *knew* why I felt better.

The lung specialist had performed the surgery, but it was the Master Physician who had intervened on my behalf and healed me.

I could end this testimony here, but there's more.

Fifteen years following my lung surgery, I found myself once again experiencing pain and shortness of breath, and wanted to make sure there were no problems with my remaining right lung. Sitting in a doctor's office, as a physician read over my prior medical reports, he asked me what type of cancer I had been treated for. He broke the news to me that the lung tumor had not been benign, as I had been led to believe so many years ago. He stated matter-of-factly, and showed me the report, where the tumor had been malignant and the surgery had been for lung cancer.

The lung specialist questioned me regarding what type of "treatments" I had received after the surgery. He shook his head in disbelief when I told him I had not received any treatments—chemotherapy, radiation, nor anti-cancer drugs of any type. He was stunned at how well I had progressed after all these years with neither follow-ups nor treatments of any kind.

As I left the doctor's office, I was in disbelief. In the following days, I experienced what others who have been given a cancer diagnosis go through: a gamut of emotions, from grief to denial to anger. I simply could not believe that this diagnosis had been kept from me for all these years; but then God spoke to my heart. He showed me how I would have lived my life so differently, without hope and with a fear that the cancer would eventually return. I would certainly not have used my life in service for Him, nor would I ever had given birth to my second daughter. Life would just be too uncertain.

It was for God's glory that I found out about this cancer so many years later—it would serve as a positive testimony of His healing power!

At that moment, I thought about that night in that small Pentecostal church when God came on the scene and healed my body. Little had I realized at that time but God had not only sped up the surgery recuperation process, but He had rid my body completely of cancer; and my life has never been the same!

All of us have moments in our lives when we want to escape from life's problems. We find ourselves like

David in Psalm 55:6: *"Oh, that I had the wings of a dove! I would fly away and be at rest."*

God *does* have our best interests at heart, even when there seems to be no answer. When we place our cares upon Him, He will make a way for our escape.

When your faith is tested, may my personal testimony of this encounter with Jesus serve to encourage you to lean upon the Lord and count on Him to bring you through. As it so aptly says of God in Psalm 59:16: *"For you are my fortress, my refuge in time of trouble."*

TO GOD BE THE GLORY.

PART III

THE "ULTIMATE" ENCOUNTER

For the final chapter of this book, I have asked my husband, Jim, to share a testimony of his encounter with Jesus. Through his sharing, you are invited, if you have never done so, to accept Jesus Christ as your personal Savior, which can only be described as the **ultimate encounter** of your life: a life that will never be the same.

Jim writes:

We all encounter many things throughout our lives; some good and others not so good. Many times, our encounters are the result of seeking out those things that will satisfy us and bring us happiness.

We look for that happiness in many different places: as children, perhaps it was a favorite toy or a new bike; later in life, it might be a girlfriend or boyfriend, maybe a new car or an exciting new career, but dating couples break up and go their separate ways. The new car eventually wears out, and careers become routine and the excitement drifts away.

There was a king whose name was Solomon. He was very wise and very rich, but despite all of his wisdom and his wealth he came to the conclusion that it was all vanity.

If that is the case, then where can we find real happiness? Maybe happiness is not what we're truly seeking. Suppose what we truly want is to be content; what will bring you contentment?

For myself, I discovered that contentment in the summer of 1973. Through a series of circumstances, I found myself attending a prayer meeting on Saturday evenings. Now I was raised Catholic and had never been to a prayer meeting before in my life, but there was a girl who invited me, so I did what any fourteen-year-old boy would do: I went. It was there that I heard for the first time the answer to my search for contentment. It turned out that the answer was not in things, but in a person. My contentment was found in Jesus Christ.

Earlier, I mentioned that I was brought up as a Roman Catholic. I believed in God and I believed in Jesus Christ. What I didn't believe was that I could have a personal relationship with Jesus and, that through this relationship, I could finally find contentment and peace.

This relationship gave me a new perspective on life. Yes, even as a fourteen-year-old boy, I began to see things differently. I began to realize God's love for me was not dependent on how good I was, but rather on how good and great God was. I discovered the reason that Jesus, a truly righteous and sinless man, died a criminal's death on a Roman cross was to pay for my personal sins. I found that Jesus Christ exchanged my sins for His righteousness. That the punishment I should have received was instead placed on Jesus at the cross; that was **my** ultimate encounter.

It's also an encounter that has been the life story of countless others throughout the centuries.

Returning to my earlier question: "What will bring you contentment?" Will it be that new car or more money? In the Bible, one of Jesus' friends records these words of Jesus for us:

> *Don't store up for yourselves treasures on earth, where moth or rust destroy, and where thieves break in and steal, But store up for yourselves treasures in heaven, where moth and rust do not destroy and where thieves do not break in and steal. For where your treasure is, there will your heart be also"* (Matthew 6:19-21).

Now don't get me wrong; there's nothing wrong with having nice things. We all desire to live a comfortable life and no one, not even God I believe, would find fault with that. However, there must be more to life than the "stuff" we accumulate. Life is so much more than retirement funds and a beautiful home.

Once again, the words of Jesus provide a view of what real contentment looks like: *"Come to me, all you who are weary and burdened, and I will give you rest. Take my yoke upon you and learn from me, for I am gentle and humble in heart and you will find rest for your souls. For my yoke is easy and my burden is light"* (Matt. 11:28-30).

Are you desiring a place away from the weariness and burdens of life? You can find those things in Christ alone. Only He can satisfy the emptiness you face; the emptiness we all face.

The journey to true fulfillment begins by simply recognizing that you were created by God to be in relationship with Him. The problem is that we're separated from God by sin. Sin is simply not meeting the righteous standard that God has established. The apostle Paul, in Romans, tells us: *"for all have sinned and fall short of the glory of God"* (Rom. 3:23).

God is perfect, holy and altogether righteous, and we're not. Even the most moral person has been tainted by sin.

What we really need is a way to bridge this "sin gap", which exists between us and God. Who can build that bridge? The good news is that the bridge has already been built.

God determined long ago that His relationship with us was so important to Him that He made a way to repair the brokenness that sin brought into the world. God sent His only son, Jesus Christ, to do what you and I couldn't: live a perfect, sinless life. Jesus then offered Himself up as a sacrifice to pay for our sins, but Jesus didn't stop there. A dead, moral teacher who lived a sinless life couldn't restore us to God. Jesus is more than a good, moral teacher; He's more than a miracle worker. He's God. Jesus not only had the power to lay down His life, but to take it up again. Jesus rose from the dead, defeating the power of sin and death once and for all. It's that single act that allows us to be restored to a right relationship with God.

You might be thinking: "Okay, so what's the catch? What do I need to do?" The answer to that question is likely to shock you. That fact is that Christ has already done it for you. He's already paid the price and, to be honest, it's something that you can't do by yourself.

Years ago, I had the opportunity to attend seminary in Orlando, Florida. One day in class, I described salvation to a professor like this: *"A person had fallen out of a boat in the middle of a lake. Someone threw a life line to this person and if that individual could only reach out and take hold of the life line, he/she would be spared."*

The professor quickly responded, *"No, Mr. Brown, that is NOT right. This person has not just fallen out of a boat, he/she is lying at the bottom of the lake and he/she's dead!"*

The professor, of course, was right. The apostle Paul demonstrates in his letter to the Ephesians: *"But because of his great love for us, God, who is rich in mercy, made us alive in Christ even when we were dead in our transgressions, it is by grace you have been saved"* (Eph. 2:4-5).

Paul goes on to emphasize this point a few verses later: *"For it is by grace are you saved, through faith — and this not from yourselves, it is the gift of God – not by works, so that no one can boast"* (Eph. 2:8-9).

Perhaps you are reading this and have never personally experienced God's grace, but desire to do so. If so, let me share how you can begin that journey.

First, admit that you're a sinner. By the way, that's not difficult to do because we are all sinners. In fact, the Bible tells us *"for all have sinned and fall short of the glory of God"* (Romans 3:23). God IS perfect and none of us can ever measure up to that perfection; that's what we call **sin**.

Second, believe in your heart that Jesus paid the penalty for your sins.

And finally, make that belief a reality by confessing that Jesus Christ is Lord and that He is the only way to pay the penalty for your sins.

If you believe that the price that Jesus paid on the cross for the sins of the world includes your sins, and if you accept that as truth, you're on your way to the Ultimate Encounter.

You will discover that your life will NEVER be the same again.

BIBLIOGRAPHY

Leprosy: Symptoms, Treatments, History and Causes, http://www.webmd.com

Webster's New World Dictionary and Thesaurus, Second Edition, Wiley Publishing, 2002.

ABOUT THE AUTHOR

Jacquelin McCall Brown (Jackie) is a Board-Certified Biblical Counselor from Light University, a member of the American Association of Christian Counselors and a graduate of the University of the Cumberlands. Her passion is encouraging others and she strives to achieve that through her writing. Over the years she has written articles for several denominational publications. She and her husband live in Northern Virginia.

CPSIA information can be obtained
at www.ICGtesting.com
Printed in the USA
FFOW01n1938311017
41762FF